Sunset Liminal

Fall 2015
Volume 2

I0191401

Poetry Editor
Greg Scheiber

Fiction Editor
Stephen Krzyzanowski

Managing Editor
Kate Gulden

Cover Art "Where, From Here"
by Theresa Moir

Sunset Liminal Press Logo by Chris Balzano

ISBN:0692546685

ISBN–13:9780692546680

Published in Silver Spring, Maryland by Sunset Liminal Press

Letter from the Editor

Dearest Readers,

Let us not forget why we are here. As I immersed myself in submissions from friends, colleagues, and strangers anonymously mixed together, we were all united in the endeavor to better ourselves through the joy of literature. The fun I had wading into this pool of prose and poetry is reason enough for us to set pen to page, be it black or red. When we write, we dissolve a little bit of ourselves into that ink on the page. When we read, we sop up that spilled sense of what some might call the soul. We have come here with ambition, we have come here with passion, we have come here separately and arrived together. And when I look around, I'm glad of my company. Never let your relationship with literature lose its luster. Keep writing. Keep reading. Keep having fun.

I would like to thank the writers who have seen and beautifully and dutifully recreated vivid scenes from a myriad of landscapes – the beach, a river, an altar to the dead. Just as a theme of water flows through this issue, the liminality of experience has washed behind the eyes of our authors, flowed through their beings, and poured forth to the page.

Steve Krzyzanowski
Prose Editor

Table of Contents

Poetry

Prose

Regina Anoir lives in rural Missouri with her family. She studied foreign language pedagogy and has taught elementary and middle school. This is her first publication.

Calaca

Your kiss, *calaca,*
is pearl.

Those cranial plates
from the earth, I dug,
needled with tattoos.

No hues stain
the underside of your fingers.

How could I
forget those hardened workman's palms
so soft

on a daughter's cheek.
How could I forget
to light your saint last night.

Author's note: Calaca is the Spanish word for a stylized depiction of a skull, like those seen on the Day of the Dead altars.

Hueco

Though he walks,
and his leathered skin
and the muscles in his shoulder
shape to the curve of my palm,
his musk has flown from him.
He has become hueco–hollowed–
the soul carved from the torso.

After he returns home,
he may perfume himself
with pulled pork and black coffee,
with the floral lather of Dial soap
and some cologne at his collar bone.

I may trace the veins of his hands
while they cool, but deep in the rigid
caverns of his cracked knuckles
that I often soothed into my own hands,
the smell of something of chicken
still lingers, and then all of that blood
that is not his blood at all.

Author's note: Hueco means "hollow" in Spanish, and refers to the sense of when a man's soul and spirit seems to be ripped from them.

Jennifer Goldring, originally from Arizona, received her MFA in Poetry from the University of Missouri–St. Louis. She resides in St. Louis with her two children and their small menagerie of pets. Her poetry can be found in *Tar River Poetry, Architrave Press,* and the anthology, *Poetry with a Dash of Salt.*

Alone on Black River

Scoop water from the river and bring it back to camp ladle by ladle. This is your exercise in patience. This is your body's movement perfected. Know there is always loss. Fill the pot. Go back and forth from camp to the river. River to camp. One trip you misstep and lose a whole batch. Scrape your knee. Bleed. Go again to the river and wash your wound. Come again to filling the pot. Within one inch of the lip, light the fire. Bring the water to a boil until it rolls and bubbles. Until it is clear and the sediment falls. Remove it from the fire. Let it cool, while you walk through the woods. Once, you carried the whole pot down to the river. Once, you carried it back full, but the water spilled over the sides with every step. You left the path mud filled, left the path pocked with your footprints. You lost the animal tracks from the night before, made decisions to change your process. Return to camp. Drink the water. Brush your teeth with it. Cook your meal. Wash your face and hands. When it is gone go again to the river. Gather again the runoff from the mouth. There are days when it feels as if it is a mile away, each time a mile. Except the time you crossed paths with the fox, then it was a dream's footprint away. Except the time you found the hollow bang of the pileated woodpecker, then you followed him through the forest and it was days gone. A ladle full. Take it again and fill the pot. Know this will be the best water you have ever tasted. Take it again. Fill the pot. One day you are lucky and the sky fills with roll clouds, with scud clouds, with plump cumulonimbus, and the rain comes. Run. Run back to camp as fast as you can. Set out all your cups, your bowls, your vessels, and capture the clear, liquid sky. Your whole camp a cistern. Wood too wet to light a fire. You soaked to the bone. Retreat to your tent, warm under your blankets. Press a dry towel to your face. Hold this pen in your hand and press it to the damp paper. Lift the full cup to your lips. Listen to the rain fill everything. Listen to the rain erase this morning's trek. Remember to forget the old process. Know this is definitely the best water will ever taste.

Brendan Raleigh is a senior English major at Gettysburg College. He is Editor-in-Chief of the college's student newspaper and has worked as a contributing writer for *Celebrate Gettysburg* magazine and *Frederick Gorilla* magazine.

Casting Sunfish

It is a small altar,
soft and wet and fluid.
But on this muddy bank, we lie
these slick, pocketable suns,
returning them to the rippling sky below --
sacrifices of mercy and
prayers to find more preferable prey
at the ends of our hooks.

The next cast comes back
as a tangled haul of
hard, dry brush.
A blade from the box
dives, snips, and frees
the sticks dangling on the snare.

And then another
little sun appears --
small and spiny,
with its bloating,
undulant mail links --
and fills its guts (now risen and cresting)

with c–shaped stainless steel.

I feel a dip and pull.
The sun rises with the run of the reel
and becomes
a final sacrifice
for the last few minutes of the morning:
a swift and fateful sunrise
just before the sunrise.

Merissa Cope is currently a junior studying sociology at Emory University in Atlanta, GA. When she's not at class, she's either at the rock climbing wall or sleeping. She would like to thank her boyfriend for his continued support, and is honored to be featured in *Sunset Liminal*.

Go Lightly Among Her

She is a circus when you hug her,
cotton candy threaded all throughout her spine.
The bandstand plays in her whisper…
you can hear
her fingerprints like fire on your skin.
I wonder if you've tasted her?
She is pop rocks and warm soda.
She is the warmth
of the lions breath on the top of your head.

Step right up, Holly Golightly. You are about to witness yourself unfurling
    with the opening
of the big top.
You've been married before haven't you, Holly dear?
You know the drill. City Hall is crying out.
Raise your flute, your bowl, your tumbler…

But she is not that girl. Her shoes are solidly dry
She is allergic to cats.

The airplane calls to her, the man–firing
gun already has her name painted on its barrel.

She will squeeze herself between those metal walls
and fall
asleep inside the explosion.
Dry shoes make for a dry house.
Or is it the other way around?
She is allergic to cats so they are allergic to her.
I ask her if that's how it works

3 for 5. 6 for 11. comeovacomeovacomeova test your luck.

The green flags of prayer are not enough. They are brittle and bruised.
They will not heal you.
He knows
as well as she
or you
or I:
luck has nothing to do with it.

Her tender, dissolving
spine melts when I touch it.
If only I didn't try to touch so hard.
She is strong but her ribcage falls loose
all the same.
She twists backward in the mirror
with her sinew like a corset
tries to restring those ribs
what a racket

She claws the sky and tastes jet–streams and nightshade
under her fingernails when she's nervous.

But who loves the lovers?

There will be a day when I won't cry
when I think
of how she dissolved when I got too close,
of how she made a mess of me.

She is not cotton candy,
not just.

Erin McAuley was born in the western mountains and raised on a hand-shaped peninsula. After moving to the Crossroads of America to study English and Latin, she embarked on a career in the design and print-on-demand publishing industry. In 2012 she returned to the mitten and founded Impluvium Studios as an independent venture. When she's not helping other artists and writers with their own creative goals, she's out exploring the woods and waters. She loves to write stories and play with ink, pencil, and pixels.

Sparks on the Tongue

Every morning he followed the silhouettes of the fishermen through the misty rain of pre-dawn as they wove their way through the old village and down to the docks. At a certain point, where a warm yellow light in a café window beckoned him, their paths always diverged. Until that point, he trailed in their wake as though inexorably drawn by the rolling gait of their passage. They towered somehow in the grey half light, strong and real in a way he didn't entirely understand. Following them, he sometimes felt like a kid chasing on the heels of his parents—although he was pretty sure most of the weather-hardened figures were his age or younger. One or two might have borne some passing resemblance to the cliché cartoons printed on boxes of fish sticks; but the majority of them were just like him. Unremarkable. Average. He never could figure out why he held them in such awe.

He wasn't particularly interested in riddling it out, either.

This morning he was tucked into a familiar daydream as he walked, hands in his pockets and head bowed as the images bloomed inside his mind. This one was about a girl standing on a wind-torn cliffside. She was wearing a flowing dress and watching the whitecaps roll in as a storm approached. He'd conjured her up before, of course, but he liked to change the details to suit his mood. Sometimes her hair was loose and sometimes it was braided with flowers; sometimes she wore white and sometimes her skirts were the same ragged grey as the clouds. Today her hair was pulled back and her dress was blue. She was pensive, waiting; her eyes fixed on the middle distance. She was watching something inside her own head more than anything else, and he imagined she came to that spot to wait for him.

It was a terribly poetic scene filled with drama and longing. It was one of his favorites. All except for the end, of course, when she inevitably became aware of him and told him to fuck off. He didn't know how or why she did that. In theory, she was nothing more than the stuff of his own wishful thinking. He should have been able to manufacture a sweeter reaction; but, without fail, she always dismissed him.

Maybe it was his subconscious trying to tell him something. He didn't know. Psychology wasn't his thing.

When it bothered him, which it sometimes did, there were plenty of other daydreams he used to console himself. Like the one where he was standing atop a skyscraper, ready to jump into action to save some urban hellscape from post-apocalyptic destruction. He'd been playing that one over in his head since he was six. Or the one where he was invisible and hitched rides on the wings of airplanes throughout history, like the Wright brothers' first flight, WWII bombers, or that plane from the *Twilight Zone* episode with William Shatner. (Sometimes he helped dispatch the gremlin sabotaging the plane. Sometimes he didn't.) Today he chose something simpler: a winter soak in a mountain hot spring—steam curling off the scalding water as snowflakes drifted lazily through the air. He imagined the prickling heat and refreshing cold wringing out every last bit of tension as he basked in the isolated terrain. He liked that one a lot, and would have liked it even better if he could afford to make it a reality.

In truth, his extravagances mostly amounted to a daily cup of coffee.

He drifted into the Pridian Perks Café well before the tourists had started to stir, the same as he did every day. The front door was heavy and had a weathered copper knob and, behind it, there was a screen door that shrieked and clacked when he came in. The shop was an artsy place with mixed-and-matched antique furniture, vintage art, seasonal flowers, and hand-painted signs. It faced the harbor and he always enjoyed his drink in his usual spot: a table by the front window, where, on clear days, he had a view of the fishermen rigging their vessels. It was a comfortable habit and he had been a regular there long enough that the owner openly ribbed him about being a performance piece.

"I'm not payin' yah, though," the owner would add, as though he'd come up with the world's most clever joke.

"Of course not." He followed their daily script and indulged the owner with a tight-lipped smile. Then he sat hunched over his drink with fogged glasses, his legs splayed out under the table. Sipping slowly, he would set his mind back to unravelling his daydreams and lose himself there for hours if he had nowhere else to be.

Most days he had nowhere else to be.

Today he had nowhere else to be.

The grey day lightened as the sun came up behind heavy clouds. The weather must not have been as threatening as it seemed, because the fishing boats were well beyond the horizon when the screen door squealed again and the frame thumped shut. A draft of air puffed inside, carrying the scent of damp earth, brine, and the mid–September chill that promised deeper cold soon to come.

He paid the newcomer no mind. He never did; but heavy footsteps paused and then tromped over to his table.

"Danny?" The woman's voice was rich, accented gravel. Familiar in a vague kind of way.

"Daniel," he corrected without looking up.

"Daniel Werner, then, is it?" the woman demanded, but not unkindly. "You were in my class 'Lions and Scarecrows of Literature.' Ten weeks you had before you dropped it."

Daniel risked a glance over the dark rims of his glasses. The stooped but strong woman peered at him intently with pale eyes. Her hair was curled and dyed. She wore gold and pearls, and had red, red lipstick.

"Yeah, that was a long time ago, Mrs.... ?" Daniel trailed off. It had been more than a decade since his last college courses. He'd be damned if he could remember the names of the professors who taught the classes he'd actually *liked*.

"Professor Trelles," she said. "I never married but for my work."

"Professor Trelles," he echoed. "Sorry," he added offhand. He wasn't sure whether he was apologizing for forgetting her name or dropping her class or both. He knew his tone lacked a certain sincerity; but there it was. She could take it or leave it. He couldn't have been the only student to drop one of her courses.

He turned back to his inner musings, expecting she would go back to whatever business had brought her there in the first place. Instead, she seemed to sink into her weight and take root on the spot.

"It was a shame," she said. "Such a shame. I liked your papers very much, some of my favorites; but you spoke very little in class. You kept too much to yourself."

Daniel shook himself out of his wandering thoughts again. "I was just a kid back then," he said. Getting older hadn't done anything to improve his outlook in the slightest; but that was beside the point.

"May I join you?"

Daniel grimaced and searched the dregs of his coffee. He'd finished a long time ago and hadn't noticed. All he wanted was to sit in peace, but it looked like that was another dream to add to his collection.

"Sorry, I'm just about finished here." He jiggled his empty cup and made to excuse himself.

"Why not indulge an old woman? Let me buy you another," she said. "Sit and chat with me. I could use some company. Just a little, mind you. I won't burden your day."

Daniel sighed internally, then made a weak gesture toward the opposite seat. Professor Trelles held up one long finger with a painted red nail and went to the counter. She ordered two coffees and an oversized cinnamon roll caked with frosting, and she brought each item back to the table one trip at a time. She settled down across from him with a grunt.

"I do things slower now, but still I get them done," she said with a self-deprecating twist of her lips.

Daniel bit his tongue to keep a sarcastic reply from slipping past. "Mm," he agreed.

"Young people sometimes offer me their help, which is very nice."

He wondered if that was a subtle barb meant for him, but she moved on without so much as batting an eyelash. And she had very formidable eyelashes. Probably fake, he'd wager.

"Tell me, did you keep on with your studies after you left my class?"

His fingers curled reflexively around the cup she had brought for him. It was still too hot to drink, but of course the owner knew his order by heart and the smell was tantalizing. He so rarely got two cups in one day, and a vague sense of gratitude welled up somewhere behind his navel. Daniel fought hard to tamp it down. Professor Trelles had only bought the drink to keep him cornered, and even he knew that was Manipulation 101.

"Sure, I graduated," he said. "Didn't find a job in the city, so I settled down out here by the coast."

"What it is you do now?"

He turned the cup in his hands. After college he had been desperate to get out of his parents' house, so he'd moved in with his aunt. She had retired to the little harbor town some years before. Jobs there were scarce, especially for someone who hadn't been born local; and truthfully he had stopped trying to look a long time ago. He mostly got by on the pity wages his aunt paid him for housekeeping, errands, and maintenance; which was enough to cover his monthly student loan payments and a handful of other bills, but not enough for much else. Certainly not enough to dig him out of the rut he'd fallen into. He wasn't about to wax poetic about any of that, though.

"Nothing, really," he said.

"It can't be nothing."

"Nothing important," he amended with a shrug.

"All work is important," Professor Trelles said matter-of-factly. She used a fork to scrape the icing off her cinnamon roll. "Always they make these too sweet," she muttered. "I like the spice, but the sweet is better with less." She cut the roll in half and gestured to see if he wanted any.

He shook his head.

"Can I ask why you left my class all those years ago?" She arched a long eyebrow.

Daniel rubbed his forehead and this time he didn't bother to hide his sigh.

"Come, tell me," she coaxed. "Or ask me your own questions. I don't mind. Only don't leave me alone for the conversation."

Daniel considered his options, among which he briefly envisioned crashing through the shop window to make a daring escape from the old hag who had captured him. The idea was entertaining, but obviously impractical, especially if he wanted to be invited back into the café the next day. Which he most certainly did. So he resigned himself.

"How did you end up here, of all places?" he blurted. The question came out more accusation than inquiry, but he could hardly bring himself to blush. It might have been rude, but she was the one who had started it.

Professor Trelles seemed entirely unfazed. In fact, she settled comfortably into her seat with the gratified smile of an instructor who had provoked the exact response she wanted. Did she frequently stalk old students and needle them about their life failures for fun, or what? "I travel now," she said. "With my remaining time I go to what places make me happy. Towns by the sea are like where I grew up. I visit them again, you see, to bring back old memories; because to go all the way home is too expensive."

"Are you sick or something?" Daniel had a fleeting twinge of guilt.

"Sick only in the ways that are usual for my age," she said frankly. "Aches and pains, nothing more."

"So your being here isn't a last hurrah or anything," he said.

"No, but we can never know where the end of the line is, can we? There is no point in having time if you do not to put it to good use. Don't you agree?"

"Sure, I guess."

"But what *is* good use of time do you think?" she wondered aloud, drawing her drink close as she warmed to the topic. She blew on the steam to cool it.

"I don't know," Daniel said, looking out the front window of the café. The sea was smooth cobalt and the air was silvery with a steady haze of rain. "Sometimes life just is what it is, isn't it? You just have to deal with it the best you can, no matter how bad it is. Nothing to really do about it."

"You think so?"

"Yeah."

"'Nothing' again," she said, shaking her head. "Always 'nothing.' I wish you would say instead what you really think. That is more interesting to me."

Daniel was stunned for half a heartbeat. "I *did* tell you what I think," he argued.

"No." She waved a finger in the air as though chastising a child. "You said what you thought I might want to hear, or what you thought would make me think, *This boy has nothing interesting to say. I am done with him.* But I have read your papers and I know more is going on inside that you are not telling."

Daniel felt his face grow hot. "What if you don't want to hear what I really have to say?"

"There are all kinds of words," she said. "Good and bad. I don't always want to hear them, but I listen anyway, because it is not always the words but what is underneath them. This you would have learned if you stayed in my class."

Professor Trelles tilted her head, the deeply creased wrinkles of her face too knowing, as though she was aware of every shameful thought skittering through his head. As though she could see him desperately twisting for a way out of the magnifying glass she'd placed him under.

Somewhere in her face, real or imagined, he saw a flash of his cliffside damsel's defiant expression. The young woman's vivid eyes looked out of the old face and deep into him, scoffing at him. Her lips parted to speak, but he knew the rebuke that was coming and he desperately didn't want to hear it.

Daniel took a gulp of his coffee, forgetting that it was fresh. The liquid seared his mouth, a flush racing up his neck, and his eyes watered as he momentarily panicked between swallowing and spitting. He choked down the drink and fire raced down his esophagus to finally settle, burning, in the pit of his stomach.

He kicked back his chair and ran for the bathroom.

Bracing himself against the sink, he covered his mouth and stamped a foot, swearing softly. He turned on the faucet, yanked off his glasses, and leaned down to let the cold water rush onto his tongue and down his throat. He stayed there for as long as it was comfortable to breathe.

When he came back up for air, water had soaked his front and his face was blotchy. Had he been crying? He scrubbed his face with his hands. That might just warrant another, stronger kind of drink.

His tongue wasn't burning anymore, at least, but it was a strange combination of raw and numb. He rubbed it over the roof of his mouth to soothe it. He tested the damage. "Fuck off," he mumbled. The words felt sharp and satisfying, like they cut deep. If he had said that to Professor Trelles when she first showed up, maybe his mouth wouldn't be stinging in the first place.

A man could dream.

Daniel composed himself and came back out. Professor Trelles was still at the table, of course, quietly sipping her drink. It was probably too much for him to hope that she would allow him to make a graceful exit.

Bitterly, Daniel wondered how long her nostalgia tour was going to last. Would she come into the café every day? Tourists came and went regularly; people who had no idea what it was like to live day in and day out with the sea rushing—wave after wave, beckoning, lonely—outside their door for hours, days, years on end. Those people were all ghosts, fleeting and ephemeral. In all his years here, he'd never known one of them. He'd never been recognized.

He'd never had a secret rendezvous on a cliffside with a beautiful stranger.

And he'd never been summarily humiliated and rejected, either.

Of all the possibilities, why did it have to be an old professor intent on pushing his buttons who demanded his attention? He'd dropped Professor Trelles' undergrad lit class because she had pushed him too much then, too. Always prodding at him, singling him out, trying to get him to say something when he'd rather be left alone. Why she thought antagonizing him was an effective teaching method, he would never know.

"You are a smart young man, Daniel Werner," she said as he approached. Again, she seemed to be answering thoughts she had plucked straight out of his head.

"I really have to get going," he said in a rush. He didn't want to be reeled in again.

"Because you are smart," she continued over his protest, "you are too good at diverting your own attention from what really matters. Because it all comes too easy, it isn't worth trying. Or because you are too smart you are afraid to fail, and you think you cannot fail if you do not try."

"What—"

She held up a hand. "You did this in class all the time. You were unhappy every time I asked you to come out of your bubble. You had valuable insights that would have helped your classmates think better, would have challenged me to be a better instructor to you all. It was frustrating for me, too, that you would not say anything. I pushed and I poked and I prodded because you were too comfortable. You were too safe. *Comfortable. Safe.* These things do not serve."

Daniel ran a hand through his hair. "Look, Professor Trelles, I just wanted to start my morning with a cup of coffee," he pleaded. "I don't think that's too much to ask. Seriously, what do you want from me?"

"Tell me one thing," she said, "just one. That's all I want. Make it something you have wanted to say for a long time. Make it mean, if you must. Make the words bad. Just say them, and I will leave you in peace."

Daniel sat down hard in the seat across from her, his thoughts spinning. He envisioned the girl on the cliffside again. She was turning to him, getting ready to rebuke him, and suddenly he was furious. He wanted to take those words away from her and make them his own. For a moment, they were on the tip of his tongue. Professor Trelles had asked him to say anything, anything at all, and he wanted to say it. He wanted her to feel what he felt every time his own dreams rejected him. Maybe then she really would leave him alone.

Then his fingers brushed the cup of coffee she had bought for him. It was still warm. And she was looking at him like the next words he said might actually matter. He pursed his lips and held his breath, then let out one long, exhausted exhale.

"This was supposed to be *my* life," he said. "I had a dream. I have lots of dreams, but there was one I was supposed to be living. There was one that was supposed to be real. Maybe it wasn't supposed to be easy, but it was supposed to fall together eventually and it just didn't happen. I was smart, so I don't know why it didn't work. I was supposed to have it figured out, but I didn't. I don't. Not at all. Now my life is—*this*—and I don't know how to fix it."

Professor Trelles reached over and patted his hand, a sympathetic smile on her red-painted lips. "There, you see? Was that so hard?"

Daniel covered his face and laughed. "Yes, actually."

"But was it worth it?"

There was a flush of embarrassment as Daniel realized that the café owner had probably witnessed the entire spectacle. In a small town like this one, everyone would know what had happened in a matter of hours. But another part of him felt more calm, more settled. The part of him that was always eager to fall into the next daydream was subdued. What he said had been true, and he didn't know how desperately he had needed to say it—how desperately he had needed someone to hear it—until the confession was already out of his mouth.

"I think so," he said. And then, "Thank you."

"Come on, then," she said. "It's time for me to go and let you get back to your life."

She gathered her things and he followed suit. The screen door shrieked and slammed as they stepped outside. Professor Trelles bundled herself against the drizzle and asked, "What about tomorrow? What will you do without your old teacher to harass you?"

"Good question," he said. He turned toward the harbor as the light of a new idea came to him. "I think," he mused, "I might go fishing."

Victoria Reynolds is a recent graduate of Gettysburg College, located in Pennsylvania. She has emerged victorious with a Bachelor of Arts in English Literature with a concentration in writing. She is twenty-two years old and will remain so until March 10th of the following year. She was born in Philadelphia, Pennsylvania and promptly after being born she needed to be fed sugar water to combat her extremely low blood sugar. She blames this event for her persistent sweet tooth.

Letter to the Dead

Will you scoop me like a sapling,
to be in your palm of bones?
I will be the tree's new fodder,
your hands once marked like maps
but now smooth like riverbed stones.

I would like to turn the tables
and cut the coroner's heart
when he holds mine in his hands
too young to take a life,
let alone her own.

The underground vultures will eat me
until I'm nothing but white spindles
and a smear of blood
along the highway of my coffin,
resting softly, alone.

When he isn't doing (almost) anything else, you'll find **Gordon Moore** writing – generally poetry, and generally as deep into the night as work or the world permits him. He's also generally terrible at working his way through the trove of notebooks and pens he's picked up over the years, and occasionally enjoys standing on a stage so he can fumble up a reading of something he's written. That being said, if you've got words worth sharing, he'd like to read them.

A Journey for Two

I keep wondering:
where did I meet you?

There was a train that ran between
two towns,
the only lifeline
for either,
if I remember right.
The people in the car all sallow,
run out into rags,
looking at me.

I think you were there,
when I tried to dodge their gaze
towards the window,
towards the azure line that leapt in tandem
with the tracks that saved us from each town;
I think you were there,
and if it was a dream,

your eyes in that moment
said otherwise.

There was a great staircase.
I remember stepping into the city,
and that's what anyone might talk about:
"Where are you staying?
Have you tried Johnny's yet?
Have you seen the Stairs?

"We finished them
last week."

It was inevitable that I'd duck the cordon,
and,
the police afraid to follow,
I galloped up the sanctuous slope.

When I reached the heavens,
the pressure descending,
my lungs and liver beginning to float –
I found a stained glass menagerie,
and every star reflected in each chink
and crack and shard.

I thought it'd make for
a lovely first date,
but when I reached the butterfly exhibit,
I found them carrying a note from you,
saying you'd just left.

Shame.

And still, I felt your footprints
in almost every step I took that day.

My point is this:
I don't remember where we met.
It's a wonderland of memories;
a kaleidoscope of angles
on every entry towards escape from the world.
Every day we woke up sated,
laughing at the jealous souls outside.
Every night was an ocean of lust,
and stuffed with the sort of speech you save
for wedding days,
or nights on black beaches, alone and
considering.

I don't know how we got here,
when we got fat and
moved slow and
left these imprints, deep
into the couch.
I don't know when we started arguing
over which channels should be
bookmarked,
or when we burned all the books
in our home.

I don't remember when

the fridge went empty,
when the menus started covering its
hulking frame,
or when so many terrible things
became appealing:
a mountain of needles,
a soft cloud of pills,
your head in a vase
on the mantle.

I need out.
I need to find the land
we thought we'd missed,
to find my sinews tighten
and strain with the effort
of learning to run,
all over again.

I need out,
and I need to yell deep
into the drudgery of this place,
to slaughter its malaise,
massacre its weight.
I want to hand you a tool,
to hack and scream in time with you.
I want to shed this old grease
that coats us each day.
I want to see you as you were,
no;
I want you to see me

as I was.

If we can,
let's stop all clocks:
let's cut ties to time
and wander out into the breach
all on our own.

I hear there's a lovely bar in the abyss.
Let's become regulars there.

JM Douglas is a queer writer and painter from Northern Virginia. This spring she received her BFA in poetry. She plays banjo extremely poorly, drinks a good amount of wine, and jaywalks on a regular occasion.

Long distortion story

things here are not
the size I remember

I can touch it all
with one hand

the horizon is protracted like
a flat map of a sphere

Nancy Clark is a graduate of Gettysburg College. She likes her coffee with a little bit of milk, quotes movies and song lyrics with every other breath, and enjoys napping on the couch with her dog at home in northern New Jersey.

The Gull

I stared at the ocean, marveling at the blue under blue stretched from horizon to shore. Each wave crashed and fell, both actor and victim. Move like water, he said. He seemed to mean grace, but maybe it was a calculated unpredictability. Maybe rhythmic, maybe destructive.

If experience is formed by sensations, then I guess the beach is a mixed bag. The grittiness of the sand burned my feet and buried my toes; the constant pulse of the tide washed through me, a siren song drawing me in, a lullaby to rock me to sleep. I watched wave after wave fold over onto the rough sand and a gull drifted lazily above in search of some unknown satisfaction. To me, the gulls are a wonder often forgotten when considering the fauna of the seashore. Dolphins are intelligent and graceful, sharks mysterious and terrifying. Gulls, on the other hand, lay everything bare. They are ever present, resting on the crest of the waves or stealing scraps from the boardwalk. Plus, the gulls and I agreed on one critical point: a day with french fries is a good day.

On the boardwalk, we sat on a bench with its back tilted at an angle that didn't seem to be designed for a human. An ice cream shop was nestled beside a souvenir hut covered in brightly-colored t-shirts, and next to that an arcade. A clanging pinball machine and a Ms. Pac Man that ate every third quarter flanked the front entrance. The local teenager working the souvenir shop was asking his manager for more coins because kids kept going there for change. The manager, fresh off a phone call where he had been bitching about his ex–wife, gave the teen a hard time. Meanwhile, the slouching worker in the ice cream parlor was mopping up double fudge swirl from where it had spilled from some kid's cone to the floor. It was different than scooping, but that didn't make it better.

A gaggle of girls -- maybe locals, maybe vacationers -- were out shopping for t–shirts. One of them stopped in the ice cream parlor for a coffee. When she walked out, isolated and quantifiable, her flip flops clung tight to her soles. Her bikini hinted at a tan line, at other days with a constant sunny ease. My thigh was pale but remembered the trace of his hand. Looking back, I can still see her laugh as she caught up with her friends, but I hear only a gull's call. He slurped at the last drops of raspberry slushie and I chewed some gum to drive the salty taste from my mouth.

Under the boardwalk, he had fucked me like a bad pop song, his rhythm too standard and lacking the ocean's jazzy syncopation. He hadn't seemed to mind the grit.

Damn, he muttered as she walked by, doesn't she move like water. He thought himself artistic, but his art of choice was ever changing. I thought about which t–shirt I could wear home to cover the hickey on my collarbone.

I wonder if that coffee's any good, I whispered to myself, trying to suggest a conversation.

The only good coffee is espresso in an Italian cafe, he reassured himself.

What about that iced coffee you told me about last week?

He looked at me like he hadn't realized I'd been a part of the conversation. That was a cold brew, he explained. Totally different thing.

Any response I might have made was drowned out by a gush of bells and whistles at the arcade. A kid cheered his high score. An hour ago, the clangs of the pinball machine had been loud enough to rival his sweaty thumps. The kids must not have been very good; we kept hearing them jostle for the next play. Or maybe only I heard them. At one point a quarter had dropped through the wooden slats. Fuck, squealed a voice too high-pitched for vulgarity. A shimmer of light glinted off the coin's face before it landed silently in the sand beside me. Every move we made settled it a little further into its lost state.

Things are always getting lost on the boardwalk, I guess.

I watched him watch the girl that moved like water. She seemed to go against the current of the crowd, but maybe that's what it took to make waves. The quarter's fall had seemed more graceful to me. I can still see it, turning through the air like a gull returning to shore.

Matthew Freeman is a poet from Missouri who's had some books published and just got his MFA...

Own It

I was walking into
the driving sleet and snow
when an old lamp lit up
a ragged sign that said

    "One Mile To Meaning"

and I filled out the form
while sitting in the cracked
plastic chair and the
intake lady said no dice
but that her eyes fluttered

and the difference between me
and the Big Satanic Hero
was when I looked into the window
and got deflated when the girl at
the table put her hand through her
long black hair when her date was
in the bathroom and the candle
flickered and I was conflated with
the inside word and out and I turned
to see the caution tape blocking me
from wanting what was already my own

and I was criminal and
was almost boring, I was tall, I was
lost, prefigured, humble, heretical,
I had to walk away and say what I
had to say to the hysterical song and storm.

Christopher Alex Chablé studied Spanish languages and literatures at the University of Wisconsin, Madison. Currently he is an MFA candidate at the University of Missouri, Saint Louis. He edits *Corazøn Land Review,* and his work has most recently been published in *Bad Shoe* and is forthcoming in *San Pedro River Review.*

My Father Bore Ghosts

secreting them in pot shards, in teeth,
in the fragments of skulls he glued
together at night with Elmer's and
that pink, rubber eraser on a yellow
#2 as a brush; photographing
them on the pale blue grid
where two metallic arms jutted
from the base, each with a 75 watt
bulb and a steel dome; placing beside each,
a quarter; cataloging each one
in a little cabinet with 38 small
drawers and a few larger ones
until they grew to the size of platters.
Once, an adult woman on his table.
The house settled at night, and he creaked
in the basement hunched over those ghosts.
The floor creaked, and the crooked pine
outside of my window creaked
even in the lightest of breeze.
Long I heard them. The songs
not of woodpeckers or owls.

I told this to Jerry Longknife of BIA.
We appreciate the doctor, he said,
I'm sorry, but he's cursed.

News of a Kidnapping

you've killed him my brother begging for repast beneath
the elm tree still so brittle the vault of stars
crushed its shadow dark at rest I meditated
over samara scattered there a spiny sweet gum in my hand
how bones decay in the earth pretending lotus flowers
absorbed and fed into something else as some simulacrum
where death begets life like names of this sacred experience where
you once heard about before the rains were few and I set
the mountain of his pyre aflame with that peace
grown from brittle branches a pile of leaves that is
his body fueled as you fueled my body as I breathed just
enough for both of us to capture
this dawn this morning star fading
when the word came from someplace unknown to me

Then I Shall Be Unburied

The clay pitcher of my body buried

and stew-cooked over the bedrock coals
covered by the earth between the hills

of you. I once was painted as

a turtle shell is—each hexagon
in stillness, maimed in its flexibility

over this mound resting on the pink coals.

Holding down my face to a heat
furnacing an earthenware shell,

oxidizing my ink and copper inlays.

My mineral shell, my clay pitcher body, boiling—
the only sound othered, the popping

of mites too buried here.

Enjoyed this issue of *Sunset Liminal*? Be on the lookout for Volume III, coming out Spring 2016!

If you want to have a shot at having your work featured in the next issue of *Sunset Liminal*, e-mail up to 5000 words of prose or up to five poems as .doc or .docx attachments to **sunsetliminal@gmail.com** with either "Prose Submissions" or "Poetry Submissions" in the subject line.

If you're interested in learning more, like us on Facebook and follow us on Tumblr and Twitter.

> http://www.facebook.com/sunsetliminalpress/
> http://www.sunsetliminal.tumblr.com/
> https://twitter.com/SunsetLiminal/

www.ingramcontent.com/pod-product-compliance
Lightning Source LLC
Chambersburg PA
CBHW050954030426
42339CB00007B/393